THIS JOURNAL
BELONGS TO
AN AWESOME
GIRL CALLED

# HOW TO USE THIS GRATITUDE JOURNAL

TAKE 5 MINUTES A DAY TO COMPLETE ONE PAGE WITH ANSWERS THAT INSPIRE YOU AND SPARK JOY. REMEMBER TO COMPLETE THE LAST QUESTION AT THE END OF THE DAY.

M  T  (W)  TH  F  S  SU     DATE: 12 / 10 / 20

## I AM THANKFUL FOR

1. My family, for giving me love
2. The opportunity to learn piano
3. My good health and clever brain!

## SOMEONE SPECIAL TO ME & WHY

My best friend Ela, for always supporting me

I FEEL

## WHAT WAS GREAT ABOUT TODAY?

I received a new letter from Karla, my pen pal in Sweden. She had lots of exciting news about

DOODLE OF THE DAY!

# M  T  W  TH  F  S  SU     DATE: __/__/__

## I AM THANKFUL FOR

1. _____
2. _____
3. _____

## SOMEONE SPECIAL TO ME & WHY

_____

## I FEEL

## WHAT WAS GREAT ABOUT TODAY?

_____
_____
_____
_____
_____

DOODLE OF THE DAY!

M  T  W  TH  F  S  SU      DATE: ___ / ___ / ___

## I AM THANKFUL FOR

1. _____

2. _____

3. _____

## SOMEONE SPECIAL TO ME & WHY

_____

I FEEL  ☐  ☐  ☐  ☐  ☐  ☐

## WHAT WAS GREAT ABOUT TODAY?

_____

_____

_____

_____

_____

DOODLE OF THE DAY!

M  T  W  TH  F  S  SU      DATE: ___ / ___ / ___

## I AM THANKFUL FOR

1. _____
2. _____
3. _____

## SOMEONE SPECIAL TO ME & WHY

_____

I FEEL  ☐  ☐  ☐  ☐  ☐  ☐

## WHAT WAS GREAT ABOUT TODAY?

_____
_____
_____
_____
_____

DOODLE OF THE DAY!

M  T  W  TH  F  S  SU     DATE: ___ / ___ / ___

## I AM THANKFUL FOR

1. _____
2. _____
3. _____

## SOMEONE SPECIAL TO ME & WHY

_____

I FEEL  ☐  ☐  ☐  ☐  ☐  ☐

## WHAT WAS GREAT ABOUT TODAY?

_____
_____
_____
_____
_____

DOODLE OF THE DAY!

M  T  W  TH  F  S  SU        DATE: ___ / ___ / ___

## I AM THANKFUL FOR

1. _____
2. _____
3. _____

## SOMEONE SPECIAL TO ME & WHY

_____

I FEEL

## WHAT WAS GREAT ABOUT TODAY?

_____
_____
_____
_____
_____

DOODLE OF THE DAY!

M T W TH F S SU    DATE: ___/___/___

## I AM THANKFUL FOR

1. _____
2. _____
3. _____

## SOMEONE SPECIAL TO ME & WHY

_____

I FEEL ☐ ☐ ☐ ☐ ☐ ☐

## WHAT WAS GREAT ABOUT TODAY?

_____
_____
_____
_____
_____

DOODLE OF THE DAY!

M  T  W  TH  F  S  SU    DATE: ___ / ___ / ___

## I AM THANKFUL FOR

1. _____
2. _____
3. _____

## SOMEONE SPECIAL TO ME & WHY

_____

I FEEL  ☐  ☐  ☐  ☐  ☐  ☐

## WHAT WAS GREAT ABOUT TODAY?

_____
_____
_____
_____
_____

DOODLE OF THE DAY!

M  T  W  TH  F  S  SU     DATE: ___ / ___ / ___

## I AM THANKFUL FOR

1. _____

2. _____

3. _____

## SOMEONE SPECIAL TO ME & WHY

_____

**I FEEL**  ☐  ☐  ☐  ☐  ☐  ☐

## WHAT WAS GREAT ABOUT TODAY?

_____

_____

_____

_____

_____

**DOODLE OF THE DAY!**

| M   T   W   TH   F   S   SU | DATE: ___ / ___ / ___ |

## I AM THANKFUL FOR

1. _____
2. _____
3. _____

## SOMEONE SPECIAL TO ME & WHY

_____

**I FEEL**  ☐  ☐  ☐  ☐  ☐  ☐

## WHAT WAS GREAT ABOUT TODAY?

_____

_____

_____

_____

_____

**DOODLE OF THE DAY!**

| M T W TH F S SU | DATE: ___ / ___ / ___ |
| --- | --- |

## I AM THANKFUL FOR

1. _____
2. _____
3. _____

## SOMEONE SPECIAL TO ME & WHY

_____

## I FEEL

☐ ☐ ☐ ☐ ☐ ☐

## WHAT WAS GREAT ABOUT TODAY?

_____
_____
_____
_____
_____

DOODLE OF THE DAY!

M   T   W   TH   F   S   SU        DATE: ___/___/___

## I AM THANKFUL FOR

1. _____
2. _____
3. _____

## SOMEONE SPECIAL TO ME & WHY

_____

## I FEEL

## WHAT WAS GREAT ABOUT TODAY?

_____
_____
_____
_____
_____

DOODLE OF THE DAY!

M  T  W  TH  F  S  SU     DATE: ___ / ___ / ___

## I AM THANKFUL FOR

1. _____
2. _____
3. _____

## SOMEONE SPECIAL TO ME & WHY

_____

## I FEEL

☐ ☐ ☐ ☐ ☐ ☐

## WHAT WAS GREAT ABOUT TODAY?

_____
_____
_____
_____
_____

DOODLE OF THE DAY!

## M  T  W  TH  F  S  SU     DATE: ___/___/___

### I AM THANKFUL FOR

1. _____
2. _____
3. _____

### SOMEONE SPECIAL TO ME & WHY

_____

### I FEEL  ☐  ☐  ☐  ☐  ☐  ☐

### WHAT WAS GREAT ABOUT TODAY?

_____
_____
_____
_____
_____

DOODLE OF THE DAY!

M  T  W  TH  F  S  SU     DATE: ___ / ___ / ___

## I AM THANKFUL FOR

1. _____

2. _____

3. _____

## SOMEONE SPECIAL TO ME & WHY

_____

I FEEL  ☐  ☐  ☐  ☐  ☐  ☐

## WHAT WAS GREAT ABOUT TODAY?

_____

_____

_____

_____

_____

DOODLE OF THE DAY!

## M T W TH F S SU     DATE: ___/___/___

### I AM THANKFUL FOR

1. _____
2. _____
3. _____

### SOMEONE SPECIAL TO ME & WHY
_____

### I FEEL

☐ ☐ ☐ ☐ ☐ ☐

### WHAT WAS GREAT ABOUT TODAY?

_____
_____
_____
_____
_____

DOODLE OF THE DAY!

M  T  W  TH  F  S  SU      DATE: __/__/__

## I AM THANKFUL FOR

1. _____
2. _____
3. _____

## SOMEONE SPECIAL TO ME & WHY

_____

I FEEL ☐ ☐ ☐ ☐ ☐ ☐

## WHAT WAS GREAT ABOUT TODAY?

_____
_____
_____
_____
_____

DOODLE OF THE DAY!

## M  T  W  TH  F  S  SU     DATE: ___ / ___ / ___

### I AM THANKFUL FOR

1. _____
2. _____
3. _____

### SOMEONE SPECIAL TO ME & WHY

_____

### I FEEL

☐  ☐  ☐  ☐  ☐  ☐

### WHAT WAS GREAT ABOUT TODAY?

_____
_____
_____
_____
_____

DOODLE OF THE DAY!

M   T   W   TH   F   S   SU      DATE: ___ / ___ / ___

## I AM THANKFUL FOR

1. _____
2. _____
3. _____

## SOMEONE SPECIAL TO ME & WHY

_____

I FEEL   ☐   ☐   ☐   ☐   ☐   ☐

## WHAT WAS GREAT ABOUT TODAY?

_____
_____
_____
_____
_____

DOODLE OF THE DAY!

M   T   W   TH   F   S   SU      DATE: __ / __ / __

## I AM THANKFUL FOR

1. _____
2. _____
3. _____

## SOMEONE SPECIAL TO ME & WHY

_____

## I FEEL

## WHAT WAS GREAT ABOUT TODAY?

_____
_____
_____
_____
_____

DOODLE OF THE DAY!

M   T   W   TH   F   S   SU        DATE: ___ / ___ / ___

## I AM THANKFUL FOR

1. _____
2. _____
3. _____

## SOMEONE SPECIAL TO ME & WHY

_____

I FEEL  ☐ ☐ ☐ ☐ ☐ ☐

## WHAT WAS GREAT ABOUT TODAY?

_____
_____
_____
_____
_____

DOODLE OF THE DAY!

## M  T  W  TH  F  S  SU    DATE: __ / __ / __

### I AM THANKFUL FOR

1. _____
2. _____
3. _____

### SOMEONE SPECIAL TO ME & WHY

_____

### I FEEL

☐  ☐  ☐  ☐  ☐  ☐

### WHAT WAS GREAT ABOUT TODAY?

_____
_____
_____
_____
_____

DOODLE OF THE DAY!

| M  T  W  TH  F  S  SU | DATE: __/__/__ |

## I AM THANKFUL FOR

1. _____
2. _____
3. _____

## SOMEONE SPECIAL TO ME & WHY

_____

I FEEL

## WHAT WAS GREAT ABOUT TODAY?

_____
_____
_____
_____
_____

DOODLE OF THE DAY!

## M  T  W  TH  F  S  SU        DATE: __ / __ / __

### I AM THANKFUL FOR

1. _____
2. _____
3. _____

### SOMEONE SPECIAL TO ME & WHY

_____

### I FEEL

☐  ☐  ☐  ☐  ☐  ☐

### WHAT WAS GREAT ABOUT TODAY?

_____
_____
_____
_____
_____

**DOODLE OF THE DAY!**

M  T  W  TH  F  S  SU    DATE: ___ / ___ / ___

## I AM THANKFUL FOR

1. _____
2. _____
3. _____

## SOMEONE SPECIAL TO ME & WHY

_____

I FEEL  ☐  ☐  ☐  ☐  ☐  ☐

## WHAT WAS GREAT ABOUT TODAY?

_____
_____
_____
_____
_____

DOODLE OF THE DAY!

M  T  W  TH  F  S  SU     DATE: ___ / ___ / ___

## I AM THANKFUL FOR

1. _____
2. _____
3. _____

## SOMEONE SPECIAL TO ME & WHY

_____

I FEEL   ☐ ☐ ☐ ☐ ☐ ☐

## WHAT WAS GREAT ABOUT TODAY?

_____
_____
_____
_____
_____

DOODLE OF THE DAY!

M  T  W  TH  F  S  SU      DATE: ___ / ___ / ___

## I AM THANKFUL FOR

1. _____
2. _____
3. _____

## SOMEONE SPECIAL TO ME & WHY

_____

I FEEL  ☐  ☐  ☐  ☐  ☐  ☐

## WHAT WAS GREAT ABOUT TODAY?

_____
_____
_____
_____
_____

DOODLE OF THE DAY!

M  T  W  TH  F  S  SU      DATE: __ / __ / __

## I AM THANKFUL FOR

1. _____
2. _____
3. _____

## SOMEONE SPECIAL TO ME & WHY

_____

I FEEL  ☐  ☐  ☐  ☐  ☐  ☐

## WHAT WAS GREAT ABOUT TODAY?

_____
_____
_____
_____
_____

DOODLE OF THE DAY!

M   T   W   TH   F   S   SU      DATE: __ / __ / __

## I AM THANKFUL FOR

1. _____
2. _____
3. _____

## SOMEONE SPECIAL TO ME & WHY

_____

I FEEL

## WHAT WAS GREAT ABOUT TODAY?

_____
_____
_____
_____
_____

**DOODLE OF THE DAY!**

# M  T  W  TH  F  S  SU  DATE: ___/___/___

## I AM THANKFUL FOR

1. _____
2. _____
3. _____

## SOMEONE SPECIAL TO ME & WHY

_____

## I FEEL

☐ ☐ ☐ ☐ ☐ ☐

## WHAT WAS GREAT ABOUT TODAY?

_____

_____

_____

_____

_____

DOODLE OF THE DAY!

M   T   W   TH   F   S   SU        DATE: ___/___/___

## I AM THANKFUL FOR

1. _____

2. _____

3. _____

## SOMEONE SPECIAL TO ME & WHY

_____

I FEEL  ☐  ☐  ☐  ☐  ☐  ☐

## WHAT WAS GREAT ABOUT TODAY?

_____

_____

_____

_____

_____

DOODLE OF THE DAY!

| M | T | W | TH | F | S | SU | DATE: ___ / ___ / ___ |

## I AM THANKFUL FOR

1. _____
2. _____
3. _____

## SOMEONE SPECIAL TO ME & WHY

_____

I FEEL

## WHAT WAS GREAT ABOUT TODAY?

_____
_____
_____
_____
_____

DOODLE OF THE DAY!

## M  T  W  TH  F  S  SU     DATE: ___ / ___ / ___

## I AM THANKFUL FOR

1. _____
2. _____
3. _____

## SOMEONE SPECIAL TO ME & WHY

_____

## I FEEL  ☐  ☐  ☐  ☐  ☐  ☐

## WHAT WAS GREAT ABOUT TODAY?

_____
_____
_____
_____
_____

DOODLE OF THE DAY!

M  T  W  TH  F  S  SU     DATE: __ / __ / __

## I AM THANKFUL FOR

1. _____
2. _____
3. _____

## SOMEONE SPECIAL TO ME & WHY

_____

I FEEL  ☐  ☐  ☐  ☐  ☐  ☐

## WHAT WAS GREAT ABOUT TODAY?

_____
_____
_____
_____

DOODLE OF THE DAY!

M  T  W  TH  F  S  SU        DATE: ___ / ___ / ___

## I AM THANKFUL FOR

1. _____

2. _____

3. _____

## SOMEONE SPECIAL TO ME & WHY

_____

## I FEEL

☐  ☐  ☐  ☐  ☐  ☐

## WHAT WAS GREAT ABOUT TODAY?

_____

_____

_____

_____

_____

DOODLE OF THE DAY!

M   T   W   TH   F   S   SU      DATE: __ / __ / __

## I AM THANKFUL FOR

1. _____
2. _____
3. _____

## SOMEONE SPECIAL TO ME & WHY

_____

## I FEEL

☐  ☐  ☐  ☐  ☐  ☐

## WHAT WAS GREAT ABOUT TODAY?

_____
_____
_____
_____
_____

DOODLE OF THE DAY!

M  T  W  TH  F  S  SU     DATE: ___ / ___ / ___

## I AM THANKFUL FOR

1. _____
2. _____
3. _____

## SOMEONE SPECIAL TO ME & WHY

_____

I FEEL  ☐  ☐  ☐  ☐  ☐  ☐

## WHAT WAS GREAT ABOUT TODAY?

_____
_____
_____
_____
_____

DOODLE OF THE DAY!

M  T  W  TH  F  S  SU     DATE: ___ / ___ / ___

## I AM THANKFUL FOR

1. _____
2. _____
3. _____

## SOMEONE SPECIAL TO ME & WHY

_____

I FEEL

## WHAT WAS GREAT ABOUT TODAY?

_____
_____
_____
_____
_____

DOODLE OF THE DAY!

## M  T  W  TH  F  S  SU     DATE: ___/___/___

## I AM THANKFUL FOR

1. _____

2. _____

3. _____

## SOMEONE SPECIAL TO ME & WHY

_____

## I FEEL

☐    ☐    ☐    ☐    ☐    ☐

## WHAT WAS GREAT ABOUT TODAY?

_____

_____

_____

_____

_____

DOODLE OF THE DAY!

| M  T  W  TH  F  S  SU | DATE: ___/___/___ |
|---|---|

## I AM THANKFUL FOR

1. _____
2. _____
3. _____

## SOMEONE SPECIAL TO ME & WHY

_____

## I FEEL

☐ ☐ ☐ ☐ ☐ ☐

## WHAT WAS GREAT ABOUT TODAY?

_____
_____
_____
_____
_____

DOODLE OF THE DAY!

M  T  W  TH  F  S  SU     DATE: ___ / ___ / ___

## I AM THANKFUL FOR

1. _____
2. _____
3. _____

## SOMEONE SPECIAL TO ME & WHY

_____

## I FEEL

☐ ☐ ☐ ☐ ☐ ☐

## WHAT WAS GREAT ABOUT TODAY?

_____
_____
_____
_____
_____

DOODLE OF THE DAY!

## M  T  W  TH  F  S  SU     DATE: __ / __ / __

## I AM THANKFUL FOR

1. _____
2. _____
3. _____

## SOMEONE SPECIAL TO ME & WHY

_____

## I FEEL

## WHAT WAS GREAT ABOUT TODAY?

_____
_____
_____
_____
_____

**DOODLE OF THE DAY!**

M T W TH F S SU     DATE: ___/___/___

## I AM THANKFUL FOR

1. _____
2. _____
3. _____

## SOMEONE SPECIAL TO ME & WHY

_____

## I FEEL ☐ ☐ ☐ ☐ ☐ ☐

## WHAT WAS GREAT ABOUT TODAY?

_____
_____
_____
_____
_____

DOODLE OF THE DAY!

| M T W TH F S SU | DATE: ___ / ___ / ___ |

## I AM THANKFUL FOR

1. _____
2. _____
3. _____

## SOMEONE SPECIAL TO ME & WHY

_____

## I FEEL

☐  ☐  ☐  ☐  ☐  ☐

## WHAT WAS GREAT ABOUT TODAY?

_____

_____

_____

_____

_____

DOODLE OF THE DAY!

| M | T | W | TH | F | S | SU | DATE: ___ / ___ / ___ |

## I AM THANKFUL FOR

1. _____
2. _____
3. _____

## SOMEONE SPECIAL TO ME & WHY

_____

I FEEL

## WHAT WAS GREAT ABOUT TODAY?

_____
_____
_____
_____
_____

DOODLE OF THE DAY!

| M T W TH F S SU | DATE: __ / __ / __ |

## I AM THANKFUL FOR

1. _____

2. _____

3. _____

## SOMEONE SPECIAL TO ME & WHY

_____

## I FEEL

☐ ☐ ☐ ☐ ☐ ☐

## WHAT WAS GREAT ABOUT TODAY?

_____

_____

_____

_____

_____

DOODLE OF THE DAY!

M  T  W  TH  F  S  SU     DATE: ___/___/___

## I AM THANKFUL FOR

1. _____
2. _____
3. _____

## SOMEONE SPECIAL TO ME & WHY

_____

I FEEL  ☐  ☐  ☐  ☐  ☐  ☐

## WHAT WAS GREAT ABOUT TODAY?

_____
_____
_____
_____
_____

DOODLE OF THE DAY!

M  T  W  TH  F  S  SU        DATE: ___ / ___ / ___

## I AM THANKFUL FOR

1. _____

2. _____

3. _____

## SOMEONE SPECIAL TO ME & WHY

_____

I FEEL  ☐  ☐  ☐  ☐  ☐  ☐

## WHAT WAS GREAT ABOUT TODAY?

_____

_____

_____

_____

_____

DOODLE OF THE DAY!

M  T  W  TH  F  S  SU     DATE: ___ / ___ / ___

## I AM THANKFUL FOR

1. _____
2. _____
3. _____

## SOMEONE SPECIAL TO ME & WHY

_____

I FEEL  ☐  ☐  ☐  ☐  ☐  ☐

## WHAT WAS GREAT ABOUT TODAY?

_____
_____
_____
_____
_____

DOODLE OF THE DAY!

| M  T  W  TH  F  S  SU | DATE: __ / __ / __ |

## I AM THANKFUL FOR

1. _____
2. _____
3. _____

## SOMEONE SPECIAL TO ME & WHY
_____

I FEEL  ☐ ☐ ☐ ☐ ☐ ☐

## WHAT WAS GREAT ABOUT TODAY?

_____
_____
_____
_____
_____

DOODLE OF THE DAY!

M   T   W   TH   F   S   SU        DATE: ___ / ___ / ___

## I AM THANKFUL FOR

1. _____
2. _____
3. _____

## SOMEONE SPECIAL TO ME & WHY

_____

## I FEEL    ☐   ☐   ☐   ☐   ☐   ☐

## WHAT WAS GREAT ABOUT TODAY?

_____
_____
_____
_____
_____

DOODLE OF THE DAY!

M  T  W  TH  F  S  SU      DATE: ___ / ___ / ___

## I AM THANKFUL FOR

1. _____
2. _____
3. _____

## SOMEONE SPECIAL TO ME & WHY

_____

## I FEEL

☐  ☐  ☐  ☐  ☐  ☐

## WHAT WAS GREAT ABOUT TODAY?

_____
_____
_____
_____
_____

DOODLE OF THE DAY!

M  T  W  TH  F  S  SU  DATE: ___/___/___

## I AM THANKFUL FOR

1. _____
2. _____
3. _____

## SOMEONE SPECIAL TO ME & WHY

_____

## I FEEL

☐  ☐  ☐  ☐  ☐  ☐

## WHAT WAS GREAT ABOUT TODAY?

_____
_____
_____
_____
_____

DOODLE OF THE DAY!

M  T  W  TH  F  S  SU    DATE: ___/___/___

## I AM THANKFUL FOR

1. _____
2. _____
3. _____

## SOMEONE SPECIAL TO ME & WHY

_____

I FEEL  ☐  ☐  ☐  ☐  ☐  ☐

## WHAT WAS GREAT ABOUT TODAY?

_____
_____
_____
_____
_____

DOODLE OF THE DAY!

M  T  W  TH  F  S  SU      DATE: ___/___/___

## I AM THANKFUL FOR

1. _____
2. _____
3. _____

## SOMEONE SPECIAL TO ME & WHY

_____

## I FEEL

☐  ☐  ☐  ☐  ☐  ☐

## WHAT WAS GREAT ABOUT TODAY?

_____
_____
_____
_____
_____

DOODLE OF THE DAY!

| M  T  W  TH  F  S  SU | DATE: ___ / ___ / ___ |

## I AM THANKFUL FOR

1. _____
2. _____
3. _____

## SOMEONE SPECIAL TO ME & WHY

_____

## I FEEL

☐ ☐ ☐ ☐ ☐ ☐

## WHAT WAS GREAT ABOUT TODAY?

_____
_____
_____
_____
_____

DOODLE OF THE DAY!

M  T  W  TH  F  S  SU     DATE: ___ / ___ / ___

## I AM THANKFUL FOR

1. _____
2. _____
3. _____

## SOMEONE SPECIAL TO ME & WHY

_____

## I FEEL

☐  ☐  ☐  ☐  ☐  ☐

## WHAT WAS GREAT ABOUT TODAY?

_____
_____
_____
_____
_____

DOODLE OF THE DAY!

## M  T  W  TH  F  S  SU        DATE: ___ / ___ / ___

## I AM THANKFUL FOR

1. _____
2. _____
3. _____

## SOMEONE SPECIAL TO ME & WHY

_____

## I FEEL  ☐  ☐  ☐  ☐  ☐  ☐

## WHAT WAS GREAT ABOUT TODAY?

_____
_____
_____
_____
_____

DOODLE OF THE DAY!

M T W TH F S SU     DATE: ___/___/___

## I AM THANKFUL FOR

1. _____
2. _____
3. _____

## SOMEONE SPECIAL TO ME & WHY

_____

I FEEL  ☐  ☐  ☐  ☐  ☐  ☐

## WHAT WAS GREAT ABOUT TODAY?

_____
_____
_____
_____
_____

DOODLE OF THE DAY!

M  T  W  TH  F  S  SU    DATE: ___ / ___ / ___

## I AM THANKFUL FOR

1. _____
2. _____
3. _____

## SOMEONE SPECIAL TO ME & WHY

_____

## I FEEL

☐  ☐  ☐  ☐  ☐  ☐

## WHAT WAS GREAT ABOUT TODAY?

_____
_____
_____
_____
_____

DOODLE OF THE DAY!

M  T  W  TH  F  S  SU     DATE: ___/___/___

## I AM THANKFUL FOR

1. _____
2. _____
3. _____

## SOMEONE SPECIAL TO ME & WHY

_____

I FEEL  ☐  ☐  ☐  ☐  ☐  ☐

## WHAT WAS GREAT ABOUT TODAY?

_____
_____
_____
_____
_____

DOODLE OF THE DAY!

| M | T | W | TH | F | S | SU | DATE: ___ / ___ / ___ |

## I AM THANKFUL FOR

1. _____
2. _____
3. _____

## SOMEONE SPECIAL TO ME & WHY

_____

## I FEEL

☐ ☐ ☐ ☐ ☐ ☐

## WHAT WAS GREAT ABOUT TODAY?

_____
_____
_____
_____
_____

DOODLE OF THE DAY!

M  T  W  TH  F  S  SU      DATE: ___ / ___ / ___

## I AM THANKFUL FOR

1. _____
2. _____
3. _____

## SOMEONE SPECIAL TO ME & WHY
_____

I FEEL  ☐  ☐  ☐  ☐  ☐  ☐

## WHAT WAS GREAT ABOUT TODAY?

_____
_____
_____
_____
_____

DOODLE OF THE DAY!

M  T  W  TH  F  S  SU      DATE: ___ / ___ / ___

## I AM THANKFUL FOR

1. _____

2. _____

3. _____

## SOMEONE SPECIAL TO ME & WHY

_____

I FEEL  ☐  ☐  ☐  ☐  ☐  ☐

## WHAT WAS GREAT ABOUT TODAY?

_____

_____

_____

_____

_____

DOODLE OF THE DAY!

M  T  W  TH  F  S  SU     DATE: __ / __ / __

## I AM THANKFUL FOR

1. _____
2. _____
3. _____

## SOMEONE SPECIAL TO ME & WHY

_____

I FEEL

## WHAT WAS GREAT ABOUT TODAY?

_____
_____
_____
_____
_____

DOODLE OF THE DAY!

M    T    W    TH    F    S    SU        DATE: ___/___/___

## I AM THANKFUL FOR

1. _____
2. _____
3. _____

## SOMEONE SPECIAL TO ME & WHY

_____

## I FEEL

☐  ☐  ☐  ☐  ☐  ☐

## WHAT WAS GREAT ABOUT TODAY?

_____
_____
_____
_____
_____

DOODLE OF THE DAY!

M  T  W  TH  F  S  SU      DATE: ___/___/___

## I AM THANKFUL FOR

1. _____
2. _____
3. _____

## SOMEONE SPECIAL TO ME & WHY

_____

I FEEL  ☐  ☐  ☐  ☐  ☐  ☐

## WHAT WAS GREAT ABOUT TODAY?

_____
_____
_____
_____
_____

DOODLE OF THE DAY!

M T W TH F S SU      DATE: ___/___/___

## I AM THANKFUL FOR

1. _____
2. _____
3. _____

## SOMEONE SPECIAL TO ME & WHY

_____

I FEEL  ☐  ☐  ☐  ☐  ☐  ☐

## WHAT WAS GREAT ABOUT TODAY?

_____
_____
_____
_____
_____

DOODLE OF THE DAY!

M  T  W  TH  F  S  SU     DATE: ___ / ___ / ___

## I AM THANKFUL FOR

1. _____
2. _____
3. _____

## SOMEONE SPECIAL TO ME & WHY

_____

I FEEL  ☐  ☐  ☐  ☐  ☐  ☐

## WHAT WAS GREAT ABOUT TODAY?

_____
_____
_____
_____
_____

DOODLE OF THE DAY!

M  T  W  TH  F  S  SU       DATE: ___ / ___ / ___

## I AM THANKFUL FOR

1. _____
2. _____
3. _____

## SOMEONE SPECIAL TO ME & WHY

_____

## I FEEL

☐   ☐   ☐   ☐   ☐   ☐

## WHAT WAS GREAT ABOUT TODAY?

_____
_____
_____
_____
_____

DOODLE OF THE DAY!

M  T  W  TH  F  S  SU     DATE: ___ / ___ / ___

## I AM THANKFUL FOR

1. _____
2. _____
3. _____

## SOMEONE SPECIAL TO ME & WHY

_____

I FEEL  ☐  ☐  ☐  ☐  ☐  ☐

## WHAT WAS GREAT ABOUT TODAY?

_____

_____

_____

_____

_____

DOODLE OF THE DAY!

| M  T  W  TH  F  S  SU | DATE: __ / __ / __ |

## I AM THANKFUL FOR

1. _____
2. _____
3. _____

## SOMEONE SPECIAL TO ME & WHY

_____

## I FEEL

 ☐  ☐  ☐  ☐  ☐  ☐

## WHAT WAS GREAT ABOUT TODAY?

_____

_____

_____

_____

_____

**DOODLE OF THE DAY!**

M  T  W  TH  F  S  SU     DATE: ___ / ___ / ___

## I AM THANKFUL FOR

1. _____
2. _____
3. _____

## SOMEONE SPECIAL TO ME & WHY

_____

I FEEL  ☐  ☐  ☐  ☐  ☐  ☐

## WHAT WAS GREAT ABOUT TODAY?

_____
_____
_____
_____
_____

DOODLE OF THE DAY!

M  T  W  TH  F  S  SU     DATE: ___ / ___ / ___

## I AM THANKFUL FOR

1. _____

2. _____

3. _____

## SOMEONE SPECIAL TO ME & WHY

_____

**I FEEL**  ☐  ☐  ☐  ☐  ☐  ☐

## WHAT WAS GREAT ABOUT TODAY?

_____

_____

_____

_____

_____

**DOODLE OF THE DAY!**

M  T  W  TH  F  S  SU     DATE: ___ / ___ / ___

## I AM THANKFUL FOR

1. _____
2. _____
3. _____

## SOMEONE SPECIAL TO ME & WHY

_____

I FEEL  ☐  ☐  ☐  ☐  ☐  ☐

## WHAT WAS GREAT ABOUT TODAY?

_____
_____
_____
_____
_____

DOODLE OF THE DAY!

M   T   W   TH   F   S   SU        DATE: ___ / ___ / ___

## I AM THANKFUL FOR

1. _____
2. _____
3. _____

## SOMEONE SPECIAL TO ME & WHY

_____

I FEEL   ☐   ☐   ☐   ☐   ☐   ☐

## WHAT WAS GREAT ABOUT TODAY?

_____
_____
_____
_____
_____

DOODLE OF THE DAY!

M  T  W  TH  F  S  SU     DATE: ___ / ___ / ___

## I AM THANKFUL FOR

1. _____
2. _____
3. _____

## SOMEONE SPECIAL TO ME & WHY

_____

## I FEEL

☐  ☐  ☐  ☐  ☐  ☐

## WHAT WAS GREAT ABOUT TODAY?

_____
_____
_____
_____
_____

DOODLE OF THE DAY!

M  T  W  TH  F  S  SU     DATE: ___ / ___ / ___

## I AM THANKFUL FOR

1. _____
2. _____
3. _____

## SOMEONE SPECIAL TO ME & WHY

_____

I FEEL  ☐  ☐  ☐  ☐  ☐  ☐

## WHAT WAS GREAT ABOUT TODAY?

_____
_____
_____
_____
_____

DOODLE OF THE DAY!

M   T   W   TH   F   S   SU      DATE: ___ / ___ / ___

## I AM THANKFUL FOR

1. _____
2. _____
3. _____

## SOMEONE SPECIAL TO ME & WHY

_____

**I FEEL**  ☐  ☐  ☐  ☐  ☐  ☐

## WHAT WAS GREAT ABOUT TODAY?

_____
_____
_____
_____
_____

DOODLE OF THE DAY!

M  T  W  TH  F  S  SU     DATE: ___ / ___ / ___

## I AM THANKFUL FOR

1. _____
2. _____
3. _____

## SOMEONE SPECIAL TO ME & WHY

_____

I FEEL  ☐  ☐  ☐  ☐  ☐  ☐

## WHAT WAS GREAT ABOUT TODAY?

_____
_____
_____
_____
_____

DOODLE OF THE DAY!

M T W TH F S SU    DATE: ___ / ___ / ___

## I AM THANKFUL FOR

1. _____
2. _____
3. _____

## SOMEONE SPECIAL TO ME & WHY

_____

## I FEEL

☐  ☐  ☐  ☐  ☐  ☐

## WHAT WAS GREAT ABOUT TODAY?

_____
_____
_____
_____
_____

DOODLE OF THE DAY!

M  T  W  TH  F  S  SU     DATE: ___ / ___ / ___

## I AM THANKFUL FOR

1. _____
2. _____
3. _____

## SOMEONE SPECIAL TO ME & WHY

_____

## I FEEL

☐ ☐ ☐ ☐ ☐ ☐

## WHAT WAS GREAT ABOUT TODAY?

_____

_____

_____

_____

_____

DOODLE OF THE DAY!

M T W TH F S SU     DATE: ___ / ___ / ___

## I AM THANKFUL FOR

1. _____
2. _____
3. _____

## SOMEONE SPECIAL TO ME & WHY

_____

## I FEEL

☐ ☐ ☐ ☐ ☐ ☐

## WHAT WAS GREAT ABOUT TODAY?

_____
_____
_____
_____
_____

DOODLE OF THE DAY!

M  T  W  TH  F  S  SU      DATE: ___ / ___ / ___

## I AM THANKFUL FOR

1. _____
2. _____
3. _____

## SOMEONE SPECIAL TO ME & WHY

_____

## I FEEL

☐  ☐  ☐  ☐  ☐  ☐

## WHAT WAS GREAT ABOUT TODAY?

_____
_____
_____
_____
_____

DOODLE OF THE DAY!

M  T  W  TH  F  S  SU     DATE: ___ / ___ / ___

## I AM THANKFUL FOR

1. _____
2. _____
3. _____

## SOMEONE SPECIAL TO ME & WHY

_____

## I FEEL

☐  ☐  ☐  ☐  ☐  ☐

## WHAT WAS GREAT ABOUT TODAY?

_____
_____
_____
_____
_____

DOODLE OF THE DAY!

| M   T   W   TH   F   S   SU | DATE: __ / __ / __ |

## I AM THANKFUL FOR

1. _____
2. _____
3. _____

## SOMEONE SPECIAL TO ME & WHY

_____

## I FEEL

☐  ☐  ☐  ☐  ☐  ☐

## WHAT WAS GREAT ABOUT TODAY?

_____
_____
_____
_____
_____

DOODLE OF THE DAY!

M   T   W   TH   F   S   SU       DATE: ___ / ___ / ___

## I AM THANKFUL FOR

1. _____
2. _____
3. _____

## SOMEONE SPECIAL TO ME & WHY

_____

I FEEL  ☐  ☐  ☐  ☐  ☐  ☐

## WHAT WAS GREAT ABOUT TODAY?

_____

_____

_____

_____

_____

DOODLE OF THE DAY!

M  T  W  TH  F  S  SU      DATE: ___/___/___

## I AM THANKFUL FOR

1. _____
2. _____
3. _____

## SOMEONE SPECIAL TO ME & WHY

_____

I FEEL ☐ ☐ ☐ ☐ ☐ ☐

## WHAT WAS GREAT ABOUT TODAY?

_____
_____
_____
_____
_____

DOODLE OF THE DAY!

M    T    W    TH    F    S    SU         DATE: ___ / ___ / ___

## I AM THANKFUL FOR

1. _____
2. _____
3. _____

## SOMEONE SPECIAL TO ME & WHY

_____

## I FEEL

☐   ☐   ☐   ☐   ☐   ☐

## WHAT WAS GREAT ABOUT TODAY?

_____
_____
_____
_____
_____

DOODLE OF THE DAY!

M  T  W  TH  F  S  SU      DATE: ___/___/___

## I AM THANKFUL FOR

1. _____
2. _____
3. _____

## SOMEONE SPECIAL TO ME & WHY

_____

## I FEEL

☐  ☐  ☐  ☐  ☐  ☐

## WHAT WAS GREAT ABOUT TODAY?

_____
_____
_____
_____
_____

DOODLE OF THE DAY!

M  T  W  TH  F  S  SU      DATE: ___ / ___ / ___

## I AM THANKFUL FOR

1. _____
2. _____
3. _____

## SOMEONE SPECIAL TO ME & WHY

_____

I FEEL  ☐  ☐  ☐  ☐  ☐  ☐

## WHAT WAS GREAT ABOUT TODAY?

_____

_____

_____

_____

_____

DOODLE OF THE DAY!

M   T   W   TH   F   S   SU        DATE: ___/___/___

## I AM THANKFUL FOR

1. _____
2. _____
3. _____

## SOMEONE SPECIAL TO ME & WHY

_____

## I FEEL   ☐   ☐   ☐   ☐   ☐   ☐

## WHAT WAS GREAT ABOUT TODAY?

_____
_____
_____
_____
_____

DOODLE OF THE DAY!

M  T  W  TH  F  S  SU      DATE: ___ / ___ / ___

## I AM THANKFUL FOR

1. _____
2. _____
3. _____

## SOMEONE SPECIAL TO ME & WHY

_____

## I FEEL

☐  ☐  ☐  ☐  ☐  ☐

## WHAT WAS GREAT ABOUT TODAY?

_____
_____
_____
_____
_____

DOODLE OF THE DAY!

M   T   W   TH   F   S   SU     DATE: ___/___/___

## I AM THANKFUL FOR

1. _____
2. _____
3. _____

## SOMEONE SPECIAL TO ME & WHY

_____

I FEEL   ☐   ☐   ☐   ☐   ☐   ☐

## WHAT WAS GREAT ABOUT TODAY?

_____
_____
_____
_____
_____

DOODLE OF THE DAY!

M T W TH F S SU          DATE: ___/___/___

## I AM THANKFUL FOR

1. _____
2. _____
3. _____

## SOMEONE SPECIAL TO ME & WHY

_____

## I FEEL

☐ ☐ ☐ ☐ ☐ ☐

## WHAT WAS GREAT ABOUT TODAY?

_____
_____
_____
_____
_____

DOODLE OF THE DAY!

M  T  W  TH  F  S  SU     DATE: __ / __ / __

## I AM THANKFUL FOR

1. _____
2. _____
3. _____

## SOMEONE SPECIAL TO ME & WHY

_____

I FEEL  ☐  ☐  ☐  ☐  ☐  ☐

## WHAT WAS GREAT ABOUT TODAY?

_____
_____
_____
_____
_____

DOODLE OF THE DAY!

M  T  W  TH  F  S  SU     DATE: ___ / ___ / ___

## I AM THANKFUL FOR

1. _____

2. _____

3. _____

## SOMEONE SPECIAL TO ME & WHY

_____

I FEEL ☐ ☐ ☐ ☐ ☐ ☐

## WHAT WAS GREAT ABOUT TODAY?

_____

_____

_____

_____

_____

DOODLE OF THE DAY!

M  T  W  TH  F  S  SU     DATE: __/__/__

## I AM THANKFUL FOR

1. _____
2. _____
3. _____

## SOMEONE SPECIAL TO ME & WHY

_____

I FEEL  ☐  ☐  ☐  ☐  ☐  ☐

## WHAT WAS GREAT ABOUT TODAY?

_____
_____
_____
_____
_____

DOODLE OF THE DAY!

M  T  W  TH  F  S  SU     DATE: ___ / ___ / ___

## I AM THANKFUL FOR

1. _____
2. _____
3. _____

## SOMEONE SPECIAL TO ME & WHY

_____

## I FEEL

☐  ☐  ☐  ☐  ☐  ☐

## WHAT WAS GREAT ABOUT TODAY?

_____
_____
_____
_____
_____

DOODLE OF THE DAY!

M  T  W  TH  F  S  SU  DATE: __ / __ / __

## I AM THANKFUL FOR

1. _____
2. _____
3. _____

## SOMEONE SPECIAL TO ME & WHY

_____

**I FEEL** ☐ ☐ ☐ ☐ ☐ ☐

## WHAT WAS GREAT ABOUT TODAY?

_____
_____
_____
_____
_____

**DOODLE OF THE DAY!**

M  T  W  TH  F  S  SU    DATE: ___ / ___ / ___

## I AM THANKFUL FOR

1. _____

2. _____

3. _____

## SOMEONE SPECIAL TO ME & WHY

_____

I FEEL  ☐  ☐  ☐  ☐  ☐  ☐

## WHAT WAS GREAT ABOUT TODAY?

_____

_____

_____

_____

_____

DOODLE OF THE DAY!

M   T   W   TH   F   S   SU        DATE: ___ / ___ / ___

## I AM THANKFUL FOR

1. _____
2. _____
3. _____

## SOMEONE SPECIAL TO ME & WHY

_____

I FEEL  ☐  ☐  ☐  ☐  ☐  ☐

## WHAT WAS GREAT ABOUT TODAY?

_____

_____

_____

_____

_____

DOODLE OF THE DAY!

| M | T | W | TH | F | S | SU | DATE: ___/___/___ |

## I AM THANKFUL FOR

1. _____
2. _____
3. _____

## SOMEONE SPECIAL TO ME & WHY

_____

## I FEEL

☐ ☐ ☐ ☐ ☐ ☐

## WHAT WAS GREAT ABOUT TODAY?

_____
_____
_____
_____
_____

DOODLE OF THE DAY!

M T W TH F S SU     DATE: __ / __ / __

## I AM THANKFUL FOR

1. _____
2. _____
3. _____

## SOMEONE SPECIAL TO ME & WHY

_____

## I FEEL

☐ ☐ ☐ ☐ ☐ ☐

## WHAT WAS GREAT ABOUT TODAY?

_____
_____
_____
_____
_____

DOODLE OF THE DAY!

M  T  W  TH  F  S  SU          DATE: ___ / ___ / ___

## I AM THANKFUL FOR

1. _____
2. _____
3. _____

## SOMEONE SPECIAL TO ME & WHY

_____

I FEEL  ☐  ☐  ☐  ☐  ☐  ☐

## WHAT WAS GREAT ABOUT TODAY?

_____
_____
_____
_____
_____

DOODLE OF THE DAY!